crocheted accessories

hamlyn

crocheted accessories

20 original designs for bags, scarves, mittens and more

Helen Ardley

This book is dedicated to my Mum and Dad,
Joyce and Alan Eaton, for their love and support
over the years, which has got me where I am today.

First published in Great Britain in 2007 by Hamlyn, a division of
Octopus Publishing Group Ltd, 2–4 Heron Quays, London E14 4JP.

ISBN-13: 978-0-600-61539-2
ISBN-10: 0-600-61539-1

A CIP catalogue record for this book is available from the British Library.

Printed and bound in China

10 9 8 7 6 5 4 3 2 1

contents

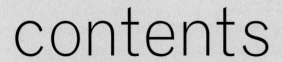

42

76

118

Introduction

Accessories can turn a plain outfit into a party piece, give a dull dress dramatic flair and generally add style to your day. However, finding the perfect piece to complement your clothes can be difficult and expensive, so this book shows you how to whip up wonderful bags, scarves, jewellery and more, using simple but effective crochet techniques.

Some of the projects are so quick and easy to make that you can start crocheting in the morning and wear your new piece the same evening, and I've included projects that use only basic stitches so crochet novices can tackle them.

From a delicate shawl in fine mohair to a chunky cape, from a beaded evening bag to a stripy shopper and from a cute beanie to a retro corsage, I've designed projects to suit many different tastes and styles, so you are bound to find things you can't wait to turn your crochet hook to.

If you are new to crochet, then start by reading the techniques section at the front of this book. Experiment with some spare yarn and once you have mastered the simple techniques you are ready to begin. I have listed all the yarns used in each project, but of course you can change the colours to match your favourite outfit. You will find that some of the projects use beads, tassels or pompoms to add a finishing touch to the crochet, and you can experiment with these embellishments to personalize your project.

Whether you are making something special for yourself or creating a gift for a good friend, I hope that you have as much fun making the projects as I did designing them, and that you keep picking up your crochet hook to make more and more wonderful crocheted accessories.

crochet basics

Yarns

There is a huge range of yarns available to choose from, in a wide range of fibres and an almost limitless choice of colours. Here is some general advice to bear in mind when choosing yarns to crochet with.

Yarn types

Wherever possible, buy the yarn brand that is recommended in the patterns. These are the yarns used to make the garments and items shown in the photographs, and they are certain to give the desired results in terms of size, tension and finished appearance.

Before you begin work, think about the qualities of the yarn you intend to use. Synthetic yarns may be easy to wash, but natural fibres maintain their shape for many years and often get better with age.

Yarn and dye lots

Yarn is dyed in batches, and dye lots can vary greatly. When you are buying always check the dye lot number on the yarn labels to make sure that you use balls from the same dye lot for the main colour of your project, otherwise you run the risk of your crochet being unintentionally stripy.

Substituting yarn

If you want to crochet with different yarns from those specified in the patterns, please remember to think about the stitch size and the weight of the yarn. A yarn might crochet up to the right number of stitches and rows to the centimetre (inch), but the resulting fabric may be so heavy that it pulls the design out of shape. Before you use a different yarn, crochet a tension square to check the stitch size and then see if you like the feel of the fabric. Cotton yarn is heavier than wool and is less elastic when it is crocheted, so always check the tension before you change yarns from those stated in the pattern.

Even when you use the yarn specified it is worth checking the tension before you begin making your chosen piece, because your crochet might be tighter or looser than mine. As with knitting, it is possible to adjust tension slightly by using a smaller or larger crochet hook, and the few minutes it will take to crochet a small square or circle will never be wasted.

The yarns that are used in the designs for this book are listed on the opposite page. All of them are manufactured by Rowan Yarns and are available from all major wool stockists and haberdashery departments in large department stores.

Wool Cotton is a merino wool and cotton mix. It is a soft yarn and has good stitch definition. It is machine-washable.

Handknit Cotton is a pure cotton yarn that has a matt appearance.

4-ply Cotton is pure cotton. This has a matt appearance and a softer texture than other cotton yarns.

Cashcotton DK is a mixture of cotton, polyamide, angora, viscose and cashmere. The yarn has a slightly hairy appearance but is soft to the touch.

Soft Baby is a mix of wool, polyamide and cotton. The yarn is soft, light and airy but reasonably bulky, which makes it fast to work with.

Big Wool and **Big Wool Fusion** are pure merino wools in a super chunky weight, so projects worked in this yarn grow very quickly and immediate results are guaranteed.

Kid Classic is a lightweight Aran yarn in a lambswool, mohair and nylon mix. It has a hairy finish and grows quickly on your crochet hook.

Kidsilk Haze is a mix of mohair and silk that produces a cobwebby fabric used single and a firmer fabric if two ends are worked together.

Kidsilk Night is a similar yarn to Kidsilk Haze, but has a strand of metallic fibre for a touch of sparkle.

Lurex Shimmer is a viscose and polyester mix yarn in a range of metallic colours.

Soft Lux is a mix of extra-fine merino, angora and nylon with a strand of metallic fibre running through it.

Scottish Tweed Chunky, Aran, DK and **4-ply** are all 100% wool yarns and come in a wide range of lovely colours.

Cotton Tape is a pure cotton yarn with a matt finish. Its construction means that it gives good stitch definition.

Summer Tweed is a silk and cotton mix yarn with a subtle colour variegation that gives a textured effect.

Felted Tweed is a mix of merino, alpaca and viscose. It has flecks of colour that give the muted colour palette a tweed effect.

4-ply Soft is a pure merino wool yarn that is machine-washable and therefore ideal for those accessories that you'll want to wear over and over.

Basic techniques

Crochet is easy and quick to work, and you will need to be able to do just a few basic stitches to make the accessories in this book.

Lace patterns and fancy shapes are achieved by simply combining some of the basic stitches, which are described below, and once you have mastered these few stitches you'll be able to make anything you like! Practise on a small square to start with, so you feel confident about holding a hook and yarn.

The first row of stitches worked into the chain should be worked under one thread of each stitch. In subsequent rows, unless otherwise specified, pass your hook under the top two horizontal threads of each stitch in the previous row. The following diagrams show the hook held in the right hand. If you are left-handed, reverse the process – the diagrams are a mirror image of how you should proceed.

Holding the hook

Two ways to hold a crochet hook are shown here: in the first the hook is held as you would a pencil, in the second it is held as you would a knife. With both holds, make sure the hook faces downwards. Your thumb will automatically rest against the flat section found on most hooks.

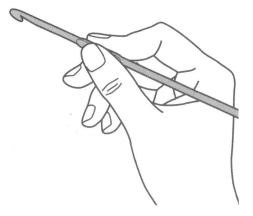

Hold the hook as you would a pencil.

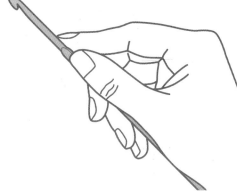

Alternatively you can hold the hook as you would a knife.

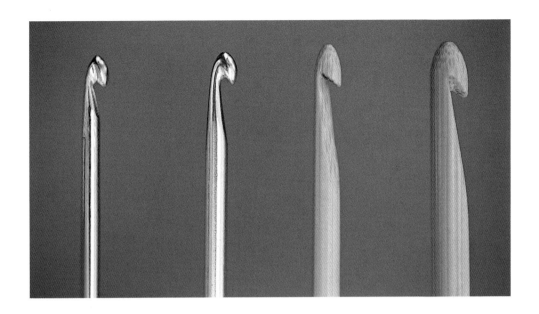

Holding the yarn

The yarn is held in the left hand and is wound loosely around the fingers to maintain an even tension as you work. To make a stitch, use the first finger of your left hand to bring the yarn into position, from back to front, so that it can be caught by the hook and pulled through the loop on the hook to make a new loop. As well as holding the yarn, the left hand holds the work.

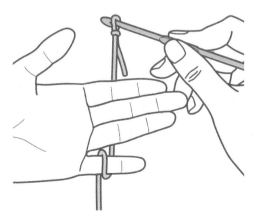

The yarn is wound loosely around the fingers of the left hand to maintain an even tension.

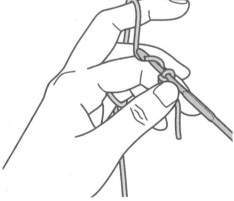

Use your left hand to hold your work as you crochet.

Making a slip knot

Nearly all crochet begins with a slip knot, from which a chain is worked. A slip knot is simply a loop secured by a knot. The knot is never counted when checking your stitches – it is just a means of starting your chain.

1 Make a loop as shown on the right. Insert the hook through the loop and pull the yarn through the loop to make another loop.

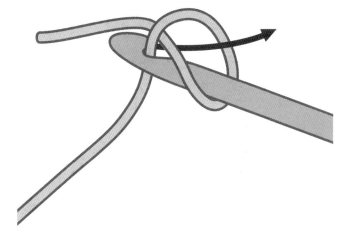

2 Tighten the loop by pulling gently on both ends of the yarn and slide the knot up to the hook.

Chain stitch

The chain (ch) is the basis of all the patterns in this book. Count the stitches as you go along but do not count the slip knot as a stitch. Chain stitches are also used to create lacy and open patterns and for starting a row by lifting the hook to the required height.

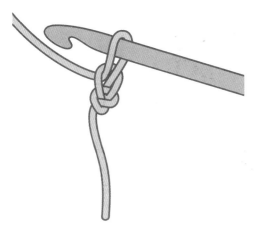

1 Start with a slip knot as shown on the opposite page.

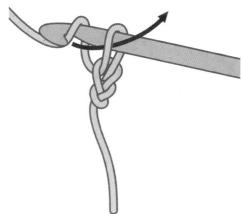

2 Wrap the yarn around the hook, from back to front, or catch it with the hook and pull the yarn through the loop already on the hook. This makes 1 chain stitch.

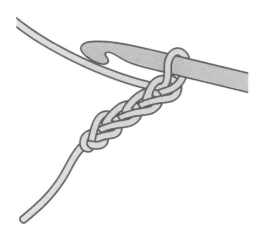

3 Repeat step 2 until you have the required length of chain. Remember, do not count the slip knot as a stitch.

Slip stitch

Slip stitch (ss) involves pulling the yarn through 2 loops on the hook. It is the shortest of crochet stitches and is not normally used on its own to create fabric. However, it is used to carry yarn over stitches to another part of a fabric and for joining and shaping.

1 Make a length of chain and insert the hook into the second chain from the hook. Wrap the yarn around the hook by bringing it over the hook, from back to front. Pull the yarn through both loops on the hook. This makes 1 slip stitch.

2 Repeat step 1, working a slip stitch into each chain or as required by the pattern.

Double crochet

Double crochet when worked on a fabric by itself gives a dense, hardwearing but flexible fabric. Each double crochet (dc) makes 2 loops into the stitch on the previous row. A double crochet is half the length of a treble stitch.

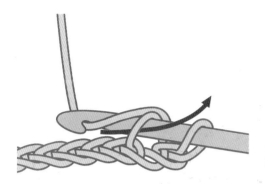
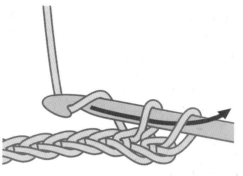

1 Make the required length of chain and insert the hook into the second chain from the hook. Wrap the yarn around the hook by bringing it over the hook from back to front. Pull the yarn through 1 loop only.

2 Wrap the yarn around the hook as in step 1, but this time pull it through both loops so that 1 loop is left on the hook. This makes 1 double crochet stitch.

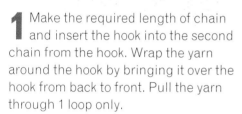

3 Repeat steps 1 and 2 into each chain to the end of the row or as required by the pattern.

Half treble

The half treble (htr) involves wrapping the yarn around the hook before you begin to make a stitch.

1 Wrap the yarn around the hook by bringing it over the hook from back to front. Insert the hook into the third chain from the hook. Do not pull the yarn through the loop.

2 Wrap the yarn around the hook as in step 1 and pull through 1 loop only to leave 3 loops on the hook.

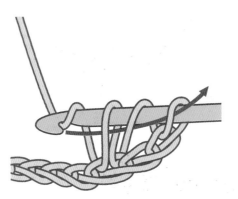

3 Wrap the yarn around the hook as in step 1 and pull through all 3 loops on the hook. This makes 1 half treble.

4 Repeat steps 1–3 in each chain to the end of the row or as required by the pattern.

Treble crochet

The treble (tr) is taller than double crochet and is used to create an open, rather lacy look which is less dense and more flexible.

1 Wrap the yarn over the hook and insert the hook into the fourth chain from the hook. Wrap the yarn over the hook again and pull through 1 loop. There are now 3 loops on the hook.

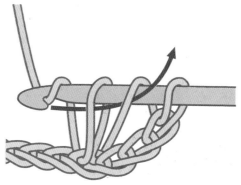

2 With 3 loops on the hook, wrap the yarn over the hook again. Bring the yarn through 2 loops only.

3 With 2 loops on the hook, wrap the yarn over the hook again. Bring the yarn through both loops on the hook so there is now 1 loop on the hook. This makes 1 treble.

4 Repeat steps 1–3 into each chain to the end of the row or as required by the pattern.

Turning the work on treble pattern

When your first row of treble is complete you will need to turn the work to begin work on the following row. You can turn the work on either side but be consistent.

1 Work 3 chain stitches. These 3 stitches count as the first treble. Miss the last stitch of the previous row, then work a treble into the next stitch.

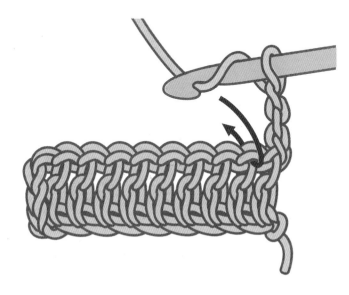

2 Work along the row by inserting the hook under the top 2 strands of each stitch in the previous row. At the end of the row work the last treble into the top of the 3 chain stitches from previous row.

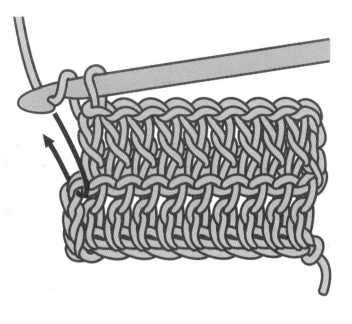

Working in rounds

When working in rounds, make sure that you keep the increases in the same position each time. Each round begins with a chain of a specified number of stitches, which counts as the first stitch.

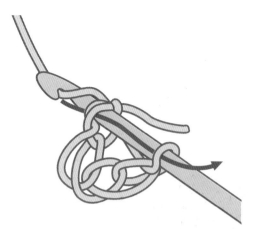

1 Work a chain as indicated in the pattern. Join the chain into a ring by making a slip stitch into the first chain.

2 Make 3 chain stitches, which counts as the first treble. The first round is worked by inserting the hook into the centre of the chain ring.

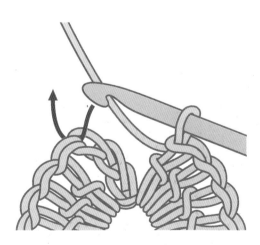

3 To join the round make a slip stitch into the top of the 3 chain stitches made at the beginning of the round.

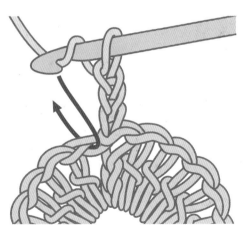

4 Continue working each round, starting with 3 chain stitches and working each treble under the top 2 strands of the stitch in the previous round unless otherwise stated.

Finishing touches

Finishing your project well is essential for achieving a successful and professional-looking item. Although the processes involved can be time-consuming, it will be time well spent, for careless finishing can spoil the effect of even the most beautiful crocheting.

Neat edges

To make a neat, firm edge when changing colour, work until 2 loops of the last stitch remain in the old colour, then use the new colour to complete the stitch.

Yarn ends

The number of yarn ends left when an item is completed can be astonishing – and daunting. A quick way of tidying them is to weave a darning needle through the wrong side of the crochet and then thread the end through. This prevents short ends from slipping out of the needle as you weave them in.

Making a pompom

Cut 2 circles of card, each about 5 cm (2 in) across. Cut a small hole in the centre of each circle and make a single cut from the edge to the centre. Place the circles together, with the cuts opposite. Use a bodkin or blunt-ended tapestry needle to thread yarn round and round the circle, making sure that the yarn is evenly distributed around the central hole. Continue until the hole is full. Do not cut the long end of yarn yet. Use sharp-pointed scissors to snip the yarn between the 2 pieces of card, then wind the long end between the 2 card circles, fastening it as tightly as you can. Remove the card and trim the pompom to the required size, using the long end to attach the pompom to the garment as directed in the pattern.

Making a basic tassel

Take a piece of card about 10 cm (4 in) wide. Wind yarn around the card about 10 times, then cut the yarn at one end. Fold the lengths of yarn in half and thread the loop end through your work. Pass the loose ends through the loop end and pull tight to secure the tassel.

Making a decorative tassel

Take a piece of card about 10 cm (4 in) wide. Wind yarn around the card approximately 10 times, then cut the yarn at one end. Fasten a short length of yarn around the centre of the threads to hold them together, then fold them together and bind another length of yarn about 2 cm (¾ in) down from the top. Tie firmly and trim the yarn to the required length.

Joining seams

There are several methods of joining pieces of crochet together, and some use a tapestry needle, while others use a crochet hook. The seams may be decorative or invisible, depending on the work.

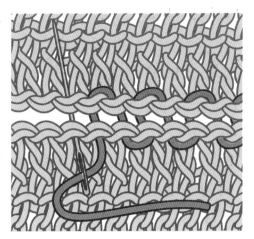

Woven stitch
Use woven stitch when you want a flat, flexible seam. Place the pieces edge to edge, wrong sides up, and use a tapestry needle to stitch around the centre of each edge stitch as shown.

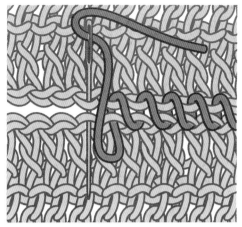

Whip stitch
Whip stitch creates an invisible seam. Place the pieces edge to edge, wrong side up, and use a tapestry needle to work as shown.

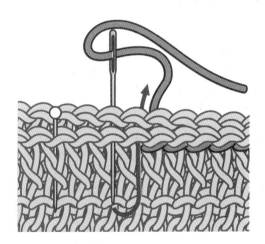

Backstitch seam
This is a firm stitch, which does not stretch. Hold the work with right sides together. Match the stitches or row ends and use a tapestry needle to work backstitch as shown.

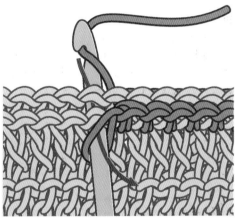

Slip stitch
A slip stitch seam can be worked with wrong sides together so that the seam shows as a ridge on the right side of the work or with right sides together so that the seam is on the inside of the work. Insert a crochet hook through the corresponding stitches at each edge of the 2 pieces to be joined and work a slip stitch through each pair of stitches along the seam.

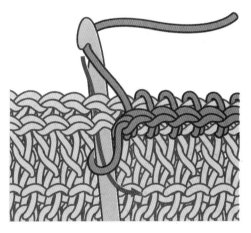

Double crochet
As with a slip stitch seam, a double crochet seam can be worked with either the right sides or the wrong sides of the work facing. Work as for a slip stitch seam but use a double crochet stitch and work under 2 strands of each pair of stitches.

Felting

If you have ever put a woollen jumper into the washing machine by mistake and it's come out small enough to fit a baby, matted and as stiff as a board, then you have felted your jumper.

Felting is the process of washing 100% wool in very hot soapy water and the wool fibres of the yarn swelling, rubbing together and matting and shrinking, creating a denser, shrunken fabric. Wool becomes felted when it is subjected to moisture, heat and pressure. In fact, if domestic sheep were not shorn periodically their wool would felt over time.

Different wool yarns will felt differently depending on the twist in the yarn. Also, the same yarn can felt differently from machine to machine as washing machines are so different. As a rough guide, an item should shrink by about 30% when felted. It is a good idea to felt a tension square before making your item to see how much your fabric will shrink.

When felting an item, sew or tack the item to an old piece of material to prevent it from felting to itself and to give it a nice flat piece of fabric. To do this, tack your item to the old piece of material with a contrasting length of sewing cotton and then put it in the washing machine. Once the item is felted, unpick the cotton and leave the item to dry.

To felt an item, put it into a washing machine with some soap and wash it at 60°c. If you are putting it into a machine full of clothes you can put the item into a pillow case. Do not use fabric conditioner in the wash as this will prevent the item from felting. Once the cycle has ended, dry the item and see if it has shrunk enough; if not, do the process again.

Beading

Beading an item can be a very personal thing. The projects in this book may be customized by adding different colours, shapes or sizes of bead. If you want to avoid sewing lots of small beads onto an item, replace them with larger beads. This will alter the appearance of the item, making it even more individual and special to you. When buying beads, take a swatch of your fabric or yarn with you to match colour and size. There are countless beads to choose from, ranging from glass and plastic to semi-precious stones. You should find a wide selection in any good craft or haberdashery shop.

When beading an item, make sure you have the correct size of needle for the bead. Wherever possible, use the yarn you have made the item from so you do not see any cotton ends. This is not always possible, as some beads have very small holes and only beading needles can be used to thread them. In this case, choose a matching cotton thread. Make sure, when attaching beads to an item, that you secure your thread tightly at the beginning so it doesn't come loose and cause beads to fall off.

scarves & shawls

Cosy cape

Quick and easy to make, but simple and stylish to wear, this cosy cape is sure to keep you warm even on the chilliest of winter days.

Size
76 x 116 cm (30 x 45½ in)

Materials
Rowan Big Wool Fusion
8 100 g balls in taupe/Tapestry 5
12.00 mm (UK 4/0) crochet hook
Tapestry needle

Tension
8 sts and 5 rows to 10 cm (4 in) measured over pattern on 12.00 mm (UK 4/0) crochet hook or the size required to achieve this tension.

Abbreviations
ch chain
cm centimetres
cont continue
dc double crochet
in inches
mm millimetres
rep repeat
RS right side
sp spaces
tr treble

Right front

With 12.00 mm (UK 4/0) crochet hook make 31 ch.

1st row: 1 dc into 2nd ch from hook, *3 ch, miss 3 ch, 1 dc into each of next 3 ch, rep from * ending 1 dc into each of last 2 ch, turn.

2nd row (RS): 1 ch, miss first dc, *miss 1 dc, 5 tr into 3 ch sp, miss 1 dc, 1 dc into next dc (the centre dc of 3), rep from * ending 1 dc into 1 ch, turn.

3rd row: 3 ch, miss (1 dc, 1 tr), *1 dc into each of next 3 tr (the centre 3 tr of 5), 3 ch, miss (1 tr, 1 dc, 1 tr) rep from * to last group, 1 dc into each of 3 tr, 2 ch, miss 1 tr, 1 dc into 1 ch, turn.

4th row: 3 ch, miss first dc, 2 tr into 2 ch sp, *miss 1 dc, 1 dc into next dc (the centre dc of 3), miss 1 dc, 5 tr into 3 ch sp, rep from * ending 3 tr into 3 ch sp, turn.

5th row: 1 ch, miss first tr, 1 dc into next tr, *3 ch, miss (1 tr, 1 dc, 1 tr), 1 dc into each of next 3 tr (the centre 3 tr of 5), rep from * ending 1 dc into last tr, 1 dc into 3rd of 3 ch, turn.

Rows 2–5 form the pattern. Cont in pattern until work measures 58 cm (22¾ in), finishing with 5th row of pattern.

Fasten off.

Left front

Work as for right front.
Do not fasten off.

Joining fronts together

With RS facing for both left and right fronts work next row as folls:

Next row: pattern across left front to last st, 1 dc into 1 ch, pick up right front, work 1 dc into first dc, 5 tr into next 3 ch sp, pattern to end.

Back

Working across both left and right panels cont in pattern until work measures 116 cm (45½ in) finishing with 2nd row of pattern.

to finish

Sew in any loose ends.

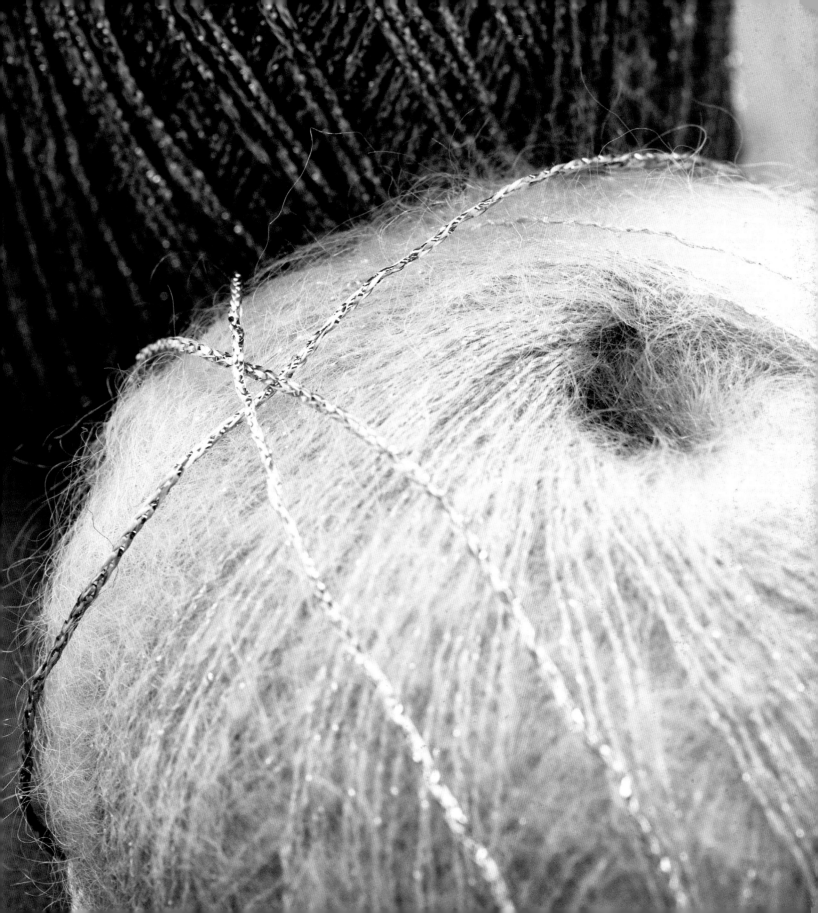

Sparkly soft wrap

Make this delicate, flower shawl a custom fit for you by crocheting as many squares as you need. The glittery yarn adds a touch of glamour.

Size
37 x 142 cm (14½ x 56 in)

Materials
Rowan Kidsilk Night
6 25 g balls in Main Shade (**MS**) grey/Moonlight 608
Rowan Lurex Shimmer
2 25 g balls in 1st Contrast (**1st C**) silver/Pewter 333
2.50 mm (UK 12) crochet hook.
Tapestry needle

Tension
Each square measures 7 x 7 cm (2¾ x 2¾ in)

Abbreviations
1st C 1st Contrast
beg beginning
ch chain
cm centimetres
cont continue
dc double crochet
in inches
mm millimetres
MS Main Shade
rep repeat
sp spaces
ss slip stitch
tr2tog work 2 tr into ch sp until 1 loop of each remains on hook, yarn over hook and through all 3 loops on hook
tr3tog work 3 tr into ch sp until 1 loop of each remains on hook, yarn over hook and through all 4 loops on hook

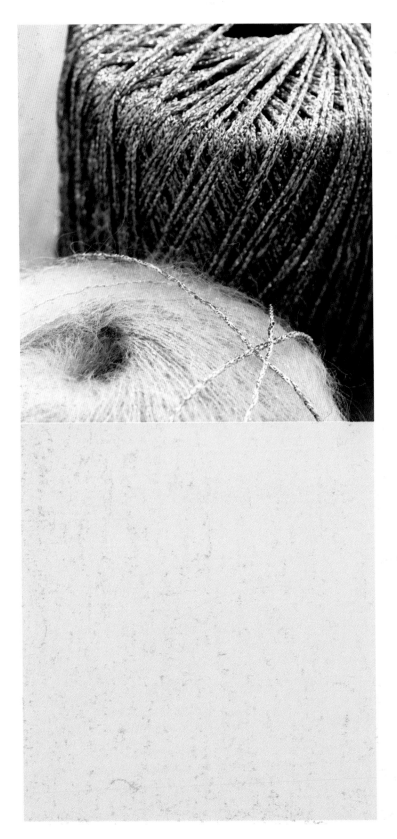

Square (make 95)

With 2.50 mm (UK 12) crochet hook and MS make 5 ch, ss in first ch to form a ring.

1st round: 12 dc into ring, ss into first dc.

2nd round: (11 ch, ss into next dc) 12 times.

3rd round: ss into each of first 6 ch of first ch loop, 4 ch, 1 dc into next ch loop, 4 ch, (tr3tog, 4 ch, tr3tog) into next ch loop, *4 ch, (1 dc into next ch loop, 4 ch) twice, (tr3tog, 4 ch, tr3tog) in next ch loop, rep from * twice more, 4 ch, 1 dc in same place as 6th ss at beg of round.

4th round: ss into each of next 2 ch, 3 ch, tr2tog in same 4 ch sp, 4 ch, 1 dc into next 4 ch sp, 4 ch, (tr3tog, 4 ch, tr3tog) into 4 ch sp at corner, *4 ch, 1 dc into next 4 ch sp, 4 ch, tr3tog into next 4 ch sp, 4 ch, 1 dc into next 4 ch sp, 4 ch, (tr3tog, 4 ch, tr3tog) into 4 ch sp at corner, rep from * twice more, 4 ch, 1 dc into next 4 ch sp, 4 ch, ss into 3rd of 3 ch at beg of round.

Fasten off.

to finish

Sew in any loose ends on all squares. Press each square following the instructions on the ball band.

To join squares

Lay out 2 squares side by side and with 2.50 mm (UK 12) crochet hook and 1st C and starting at 4 ch corner work 1 dc into 4 ch corner, 2 ch and in corresponding corner on other square work 1 dc, 2 ch. Cont working 1 dc, 2 ch into every 4 ch sp up the length of the shawl until 19 squares on both sides have been joined together.

Join the next row of squares to the shawl as for the row just worked until 5 rows of squares have been joined. Then join the squares together along the other sides. Sew in any loose ends.

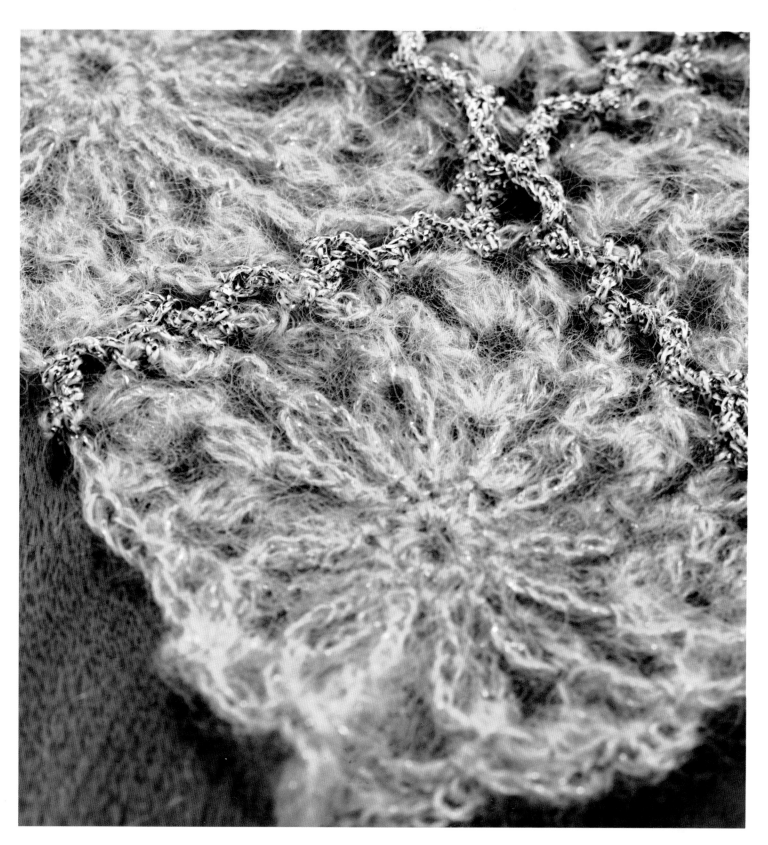

Curly whirly scarf

This funky and colourful scarf is made from chunky yarn and so will grow satisfyingly quickly on your crochet hook: make one in just a day.

Size
Approximately 172 cm (71 in) long

Materials
Rowan Big Wool

• Colourway 1
2 100 g balls in Main Shade (**MS**) bright pink/Glamour 36
2 100 g balls in 1st Contrast (**1st C**) pale pink/Whoosh 14
2 100 g balls in 2nd Contrast (**2nd C**) pale green/Pistachio 29
12.00 mm (UK 4/0) crochet hook
Tapestry needle

• Colourway 2
2 100 g balls in Main Shade (**MS**) variegated brown/Best Brown 27
2 100 g balls in 1st Contrast (**1st C**) pale brown/Latte 18
2 100 g balls in 2nd Contrast (**2nd C**) cream/Sugar Spun 16
12.00 mm (UK 4/0) crochet hook
Tapestry needle

Tension
It is difficult to specify a tension as there are so few rows in this pattern so simply work to the measurements given.

Abbreviations
1st C 1st Contrast
2nd C 2nd Contrast
ch chain
cm centimetres
dc double crochet
in inches
mm millimetres
MS Main Shade
rep repeat
tr treble

to make

With 12.00 mm (UK 4/0) crochet hook and MS make 104 ch.

1st row: 1 tr into 4th ch from hook, 2 tr into same ch, *4 tr into next ch, rep from * to end, turn.
Change to 1st C.

2nd row: 1 ch, 2 dc into first tr, 2 dc into each tr to end, turn.
Change to 2nd C.

3rd row: 1 ch, 1 dc into each dc to end, turn.
Fasten off

to finish

Uncoil the scarf so you have the starting ch in a long length. With MS work 1 dc into each ch st. Fasten off. Sew in any loose ends.

Glittery tassel scarf

A glitzy, feminine version of the traditional striped scarf, this simple stitch is worked lengthways for a more interesting effect.

Size
13 x 182 cm (5 x 72 in) excluding tassels

Materials
Rowan Soft Lux RYC
2 50 g balls in Main Shade (**MS**) pale blue/Ciel 004
2 50 g balls in 1st Contrast (**1st C**) brown/Sable 008
4.50 mm (UK 7) crochet hook

Tension
19 sts and 7½ rows to 10 cm (4 in) measured over pattern on 4.50 mm (UK 7) crochet hook or size required to achieve this tension.

Abbreviations
1st C 1st Contrast
beg beginning
ch chain
cm centimetres
cont continue
dc double crochet
in inches
mm millimetres
MS Main Shade
rep repeat
sp space
tr treble

to make

With 4.50 mm (UK 7) crochet hook and MS make 279 ch.

1st row: (2 tr, 1 ch, 2 tr) into 5th ch from hook, *miss 3 ch, (2 tr, 1 ch, 2 tr) into next ch, rep from * to last 2 ch, miss 1 ch, 1 tr into last ch, turn.
Change to 1st C.

2nd row: 3 ch, miss first 3 tr, *(2 tr, 1 ch, 2 tr) into 1 ch sp, miss next 4 tr, rep from * ending miss last 2 tr, 1 tr into next ch, turn.
Change to MS.

3rd row: As 2nd row.

2nd and 3rd rows form the pattern. Cont in pattern for a further 6 rows (9 rows of pattern in total), changing colour every row.

10th row: With MS, 3 ch, miss 3 tr, 1 dc into 1 ch sp, *3 ch, miss 4 tr, 1 dc into 1 ch sp, rep from * to last 3 sts, 2 ch, 1 dc into top of 3 ch. Fasten off.

to finish

Cut yarn into 40 cm (16 in) lengths. Using 4 lengths for each tassel attach basic tassels (see page 22) into each row-end, matching colour of tassel to colour of row, and enclosing ends left at each colour change.

Pompom shoulder shawl

A colourful lacy shawl to wrap yourself in on cool summer evenings. Detailed with tiny pompoms, it'll complement your prettiest dress.

Size
33 x 164 cm (13 x 64½ in) (not including pompoms)

Materials
Rowan Kid Classic
7 50 g balls in Main Shade (**MS**) rust/Cherry Red 847
1 50 g ball in 1st Contrast (**1st C**) purple/Royal 835
Rowan Kidsilk Haze
4 25 g balls in 2nd Contrast (**2nd C**) orange/Marmalade 596
4.50 mm (UK 7) crochet hook.
Tapestry needle

Tension
As different yarn weights are used and there is no pattern repeat it is difficult to specify a tension so simply work to the measurements given.

Abbreviations
1st C 1st Contrast
2nd C 2nd Contrast
beg beginning
bobble work 4 dtr into arch until 1 loop of each remains on hook, yarn over and through all 5 loops on hook
ch chain
cm centimetres
dc double crochet
in inches
mm millimetres
MS Main Shade
rep repeat
sp spaces
st(s) stitch(es)
tr treble

to make

With 4.50 mm (UK 7) crochet hook and MS make 296 ch.

1st row: 1 dc into 2nd ch from hook, 1 dc into each ch to end, turn. 295 sts.

2nd row: 1 ch, 1 dc into first st, *miss 2 sts, 5 tr into next st, miss 2 sts, 1 dc into next st, rep from * to end, turn. 49 shells.

Change to 1st C.

3rd row: 5 ch, (counts as first tr, 2 ch), miss 2 tr, 1 dc in 3rd of 5 tr, 2 ch, miss 2 tr, 1 tr into next dc, *2 ch, miss 2 tr, 1 dc into 3rd of 5 tr, 2 ch, miss 2 tr, 1 tr into next dc, rep from * to end, turn.

Change to 2nd C and use 2 ends together.

4th row: 3 ch (counts as first tr), 1 tr into each st to end, turn.

Rep last row 1 more time.

Change to 1st C.

6th row: 1 ch, 1 dc into each tr to end, turn.

Change to MS.

7th row: As 2nd row.

8th row: As 3rd row.

Rep 7th and 8th rows 2 more times.

Change to 2nd C and use 2 ends together.

13th row: 3 ch (counts as first tr), *2 tr into next ch sp, 1 ch, miss 1 dc, 2 tr into next ch sp, 1 ch, miss 1 tr, rep from * to end, ending 1 tr into 3rd of 5 ch, turn.

14th row: 3 ch (counts as first tr), 1 tr into each of next 2 tr, *1 ch, 1 tr into each of next 2 tr, rep from * to end, ending 1 tr into 3rd of 3 ch, turn.

Change to 1st C.

15th row: 1 ch, 1 dc into each st to end, turn.

Change to 2nd C and use 2 ends together.

16th row: 3 ch (counts as first tr), 1 tr into each dc to end, turn.

17th row: 3 ch (counts as first tr), 1 tr into each tr to end, turn.

Rep last row 1 more time.

Change to MS.

19th row: As 2nd row.

Change to 1st C.

20th row: As 3rd row.

Rep the last 2 rows twice more.

Change to MS.

25th row: 3 ch (counts as first tr) 1 tr into each of next 2 ch, *miss 1 dc, 1 ch, 1 tr into each of next 2 ch, 1 ch, miss 1 tr, 1 tr into each of next 2 ch, rep from * ending 1 ch, miss 1 dc, 1 tr into each of next 3 ch, turn.

Change to 2nd C and use 2 ends together.

26th row: 3 ch (counts as first tr), 1 tr into each of next 2 tr, *miss 1 ch, 1 ch, 1 tr into each of next 2 tr, rep from * to last st, 1 tr into last st, turn.

Rep last row twice more.

Change to 1st C.

29th row: 1 ch, 1 dc into each st to end, turn. 295 sts.

Change to MS.

30th row: 3 ch, (counts as first tr) 1 tr into each of next 20 dc, *2 tr into next dc, 1 tr into each of next 41 dc, rep from * 5 times, 2 tr into next dc, 1 tr into each of last 21 dc, turn. 302 sts.

31st row: 6 ch, miss first 2 tr, *1 dc into each of next 5 tr, 6 ch, miss 3 tr, 1 dc into each of next 5 tr, 6 ch, miss 2 tr, rep from * 18 times, 1 dc into each of next 5 tr, 6 ch, miss 3 tr, 1 dc into each of next 5 tr, 2 ch, miss 1 tr, 1 tr into last tr, turn. 40 6 ch loops.

32nd row: 1 ch, 1 dc into first tr, *4 ch, work 1 bobble into next 6 ch arch, into same arch as bobble work (3 ch, 1 bobble) twice, 4 ch, 1 dc into next 6 ch arch, rep from * to end placing last dc into 3rd of 6 ch at beg of previous row, turn.

33rd row: 7 ch (counts as 1 dtr, 3 ch), *work 1 bobble into next 4 ch arch, 3 ch, (1 bobble into next 3 ch arch, 3 ch) twice, 1 bobble into next 4 ch arch, 3 ch, 1 dtr into next dc, 3 ch, rep from * to end omitting 3 ch at end of last rep, turn.

Change to 1st C.

34th row: 1 ch, 1 dc into first dtr, 1 ch, (1 dc into next arch, 3 ch) twice, 4 tr into next arch, *3 ch, (1 dc into next arch, 3 ch) 4 times, 4 tr into next arch, rep from * to last 2 arches, (3 ch, 1 dc into next arch) twice, 1 ch, 1 dc into 4th of 7 ch, turn.

Change to MS.

35th row: 1 ch, 1 dc into first dc, 3 ch, (1 dc into next 3 ch arch, 3 ch) twice, miss 1 tr, 1 tr into each of next 2 tr, *3 ch, (1 dc into next arch, 3 ch) 5 times, miss 1 tr, 1 tr into each of next 2 tr, rep from * to last 2 3 ch arches, 3 ch (1 dc into next arch, 3 ch) twice, 1 dc into last dc, turn.

36th row: 1 ch, 1 dc into first dc, work 3 dc into each of next 3 arches, 1 dc into next tr, 3 ch, 1 dc into next tr, *3 dc into each of next 6 arches, 1 dc into next tr, 3 ch, 1 dc into next tr rep from * to last 3 arches, 3 dc into each of last 3 arches, 1 dc into last dc.
Fasten off.

to finish

Sew in any loose ends.
With 4.50 mm (UK 7) crochet hook and MS work a row of shell pattern down both sides of the scarf (as 2nd row).
Make 20 small pompoms from MS (see page 22) and attach one to each point of the lacy edge.

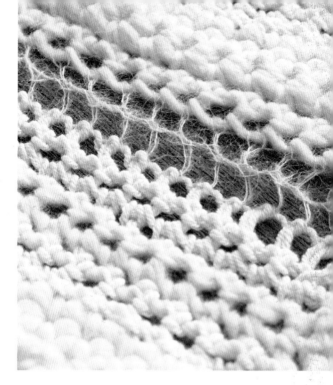

Multi-yarn scarf

Yarns of different weights – from fine mohair to chunky – are combined with a very simple crochet stitch to make this unusual, contemporary scarf.

Size
25 X 193 cm (10 x 76 in) excluding tassels

Materials
Rowan Big Wool
1 100 g ball in Main Shade (**MS**) white/White Hot 1
Rowan Soft Baby
1 50 g ball in 1st Contrast (**1st C**) palest pink/Cloud 01
Rowan Wool Cotton
2 50 g balls in 2nd Contrast (**2nd C**) White/Antique 900
Rowan Kidsilk Haze
1 25 g ball in 3rd Contrast (**3rd C**) Ivory/Pearl 590
10.00 mm (UK 3/0) crochet hook
6.00 mm (UK 4) crochet hook
Tapestry needle

Tension
One repeat of the stripe pattern measures 14.5 cm (5¾ in).

Abbreviations
1st C 1st Contrast
2nd C 2nd Contrast
3rd C 3rd Contrast
ch chain
cm centimetres
dc double crochet
in inches
mm millimetres
MS Main Shade
rep repeat

to make

With 10.00 mm (UK 3/0) crochet hook and MS make 24 ch. Fasten off.
Change to 1st C.
1st row: 1 dc into each ch to end, turn.
2nd row: 1 ch (does not count as first dc), 1 dc into first dc, 1 dc into each dc to end, turn.
Change to 3rd C.
3rd and 4th rows: As 2nd row.
Change to 2nd C.
5th, 6th and 7th rows: As 2nd row.
Change to 1st C.
8th and 9th rows: As 2nd row.
Change to 2nd C.
10th, 11th and 12th rows: As 2nd row.
Change to MS.
13th and 14th rows: As 2nd row.
Change to 1st C.
15th row: As 2nd row.
The 2nd–15th rows form the stripe pattern.
Rep from 2nd row until scarf measures 193 cm (76 in).
Fasten off.

to finish

Sew in any loose ends.
Pull the scarf into shape and press it following the instructions on the ball band.
With 6.00 mm (UK 4) crochet hook and 1st C and starting at a corner, work 1 row of dc along each long edge of the scarf working 1dc into each st on the thicker yarns and 2 dc into each st on the finer yarns.
Attach basic tassels (see page 22), made from 1 25 cm (10 in) strand of MS, to the ends of the scarf.

bags

Multi-stripe shopper

Bring colour and fun to even the most mundane shopping trip with this quick-to-make stripy bag worked in a tape yarn.

Size
34 x 36 cm (13¼ x 14 in)

Materials
Rowan Cotton Tape
3 50 g balls in Main Shade (**MS**) black/Spider 556
2 50 g balls in 1st Contrast (**1st C**) red/Scorched 554
2 50 g balls in 2nd Contrast (**2nd C**) ecru/String 542
6.00 mm (UK 4) crochet hook
Tapestry needle
2 33 x 38 cm (13 x 15 in) pieces of fabric for lining
Sewing thread to match fabric
Sewing machine
Sewing needle

Tension
12 sts and 10 rows to 10 cm (4 in) measured over pattern on a 6.00 mm (UK 4) crochet hook or the size required to achieve this tension.

Abbreviations
1st C 1st Contrast
2nd C 2nd Contrast
ch chain
cm centimetres
dc double crochet
dtr double treble
in inches
mm millimetres
MS Main Shade
rep repeat
RS right side
sp space
st(s) stitch(es)
tr treble

Bag (make 2)

With 6.00 mm (UK 4) crochet hook and MS make 42 ch.

1st row (RS): 1 dc into 2nd ch from hook, 1 dc into next ch, *1 ch, miss 1 ch, 1 dc into each of next 3 ch, rep from * to last 3 sts, 1 ch, miss 1 ch, 1 dc into next 2 ch, turn.

2nd row: 3 ch (counts as first tr), miss first dc, 1 tr into next dc, *1 ch, miss 1 ch, 1 tr into each of next 3 dc, rep from *to last 3 sts, 1 ch, miss 1 ch, 1 tr into each of next 2 dc, turn. Do not break off MS but strand yarn neatly up the side of the bag.
Change to 1st C.

3rd row: 1 ch, 1 dc into each of first 2 tr, 1 dtr into 1 ch sp of 1st row, *1 dc into next tr, 1 ch, miss 1 tr, 1 dc into next tr, 1 dtr into next 1 ch sp of 1st row, rep from * to last 2 tr, 1 dc into next tr, 1 dc into 3rd of 3 ch, turn.

4th row: 3 ch (counts as first tr), miss first dc, 1 tr into each of next 3 sts, *1 ch, miss 1 ch, 1 tr into each of next 3 sts, rep from * to last dc, 1 tr into last dc, turn.
Change to 2nd C.

5th row: 1 ch, 1 dc into each of first 2 tr, *1 ch, miss 1 tr, 1 dc into next tr, 1 dtr into next 1 ch sp of 3rd row, 1 dc into next tr, rep from * to last 3 sts, 1 ch, miss 1 tr, 1 dc into next tr, 1 dc into 3rd of 3 ch, turn.

6th row: 3 ch (counts as first tr), miss first dc, 1 tr into next dc, *1 ch, miss 1 ch, 1 tr into each of next 3 sts, rep from * to last 3 sts, 1 ch, miss 1 ch, 1 tr into each of next 2 sts, turn.
Change to MS.

7th row: 1 ch, 1 dc into each of first 2 tr, 1 dtr into 1 ch sp of 5th row, *1 dc into next tr, 1 ch, miss 1 tr, 1 dc into next tr, 1 dtr into next 1 ch sp of 5th row, rep from * to last 2 sts, 1 dc into next tr, 1 dc into 3rd of 3 ch, turn.

8th row: As 4th row but using MS.
Rep 5th to 8th rows for pattern working 2 rows in each colour until work measures 29 cm (11½ in) and finishing with 2 rows in 2nd C.
Change to MS.

Next row: Work 1 row of pattern in each rep replacing 1 ch, miss 1 tr with 1 dc in tr, turn.

Next row: 1 ch, 1 dc into each of first 2 sts, *miss 1 st, 1 dc into each of next 2 sts, rep from * to end. (28 sts)

Next row: 1 ch, 1 dc into each dc to end, turn.

Rep last row 4 more times.

Next row: 1 ch, 1 dc into each of next 7 dc, make 14 ch, miss 14 dc, 1 dc into each of next 7 sts, turn.

Next row: 1 ch, 1 dc into next 7 sts, 1 dc into each of next 14 ch, 1 dc into each of next 7 sts, turn.

Next row: 1 ch, 1 dc into each dc to end, turn.

Rep the last row twice.

Fasten off.

to finish

Sew in any loose ends.

WS facing, neatly sew the sides and the bottom of bag together.

Taking 2 cm (¾ in) into seams, machine stitch the two pieces of fabric together along one long (lower) edge and two short (side) edges. Press under 2 cm (¾ in) around the top edge. WS facing, slip the lining inside the bag and sew the top edge to the last row of the pattern.

Felted mesh bag

A contemporary felted finish and a scattering of little flowers and beaded detail make this bag a stylish and practical project.

Size
32 x 36 cm (12½ x 14¼ in)

Materials
Scottish Tweed Chunky
3 100 g balls in Main Shade (**MS**) blue–green/Sea Green 6
Scottish Tweed 4-ply
1 25 g ball in 1st Contrast (**1st C**) pale blue/Skye 3
1 25 g ball in 2nd Contrast (**2nd C**) pale green/Machair 2
1 25 g ball in 3rd Contrast (**3rd C**) dark turquoise/Mallard 20
7.00 mm (UK 2) crochet hook.
2.50 mm (UK 12) crochet hook
Tapestry needle
1 bag of Rowan beads blue/01013
Beading needle and thread
66 x 36 cm (26 x 14¼ in) of fabric for lining
Sewing thread to match fabric
Sewing machine
Sewing needle

Tension
12 sts and 6 rows to 10 cm (4 in) measured over pattern BEFORE WASHING worked with a 7.00 mm (UK 2) crochet hook or the size required to achieve this tension.

Abbreviations
1st C 1st Contrast
2nd C 2nd Contrast
3rd C 3rd Contrast
beg beginning
ch chain
cm centimetres
dc double crochet
in inches
mm millimetres
MS Main Shade
rep repeat
sp space
ss slip stitch
st stitch
tr treble
tr2tog work 2 tr into ring until 1 loop of each remains on hook, yarn over hook and through all 3 loops on hook

Bag (worked in 1 piece)

With 7.00 mm (UK 2) crochet hook and MS make 80 ch, join with a ss into first ch to form a ring.

1st round: 4 ch (counts as 1 tr, 1 ch), *miss 1 ch, 1 tr into next ch, 1 ch, rep from * to end, ss into 3rd of 4th ch at beg of round.

2nd round: 4 ch (counts as 1 tr, 1 ch), *miss 1 ch, 1 tr into next tr, 1 ch rep from * to end, ss into 3rd of 4th ch at beg of round.

Rep 2nd round for a further 16 rounds.

Next round: 1 ch (does not count as first st), 1 dc into first tr, *1 dc into next ch sp, 1 dc into next tr, rep from * to end, 1 dc into last ch sp, ss into first dc.

Next round: 1 ch (does not count as first st) 1 dc into first dc, 1 dc into each dc to end, ss into first dc.

Rep last round 3 more times.

Fasten off.

Handles (make 2)

With 7.00 mm (UK 2) crochet hook and MS make 60 ch.

1st row: 1 dc into 2nd ch from hook, 1 dc into each ch to end, turn.

2nd row: 1 ch, 1 dc into each dc to end, turn.

Rep last row 2 more times.

Fasten off.

Flowers

With 2.50 mm (UK 12) crochet hook and 1st C make 6 ch, ss into first ch to form a ring.

1st round: 1 ch, *1 dc into ring, 3 ch, tr2tog, 3 ch, rep from * 4 times, ss into first dc.

Fasten off.

Make 5 more flowers in 1st C, 6 in 2nd C and 4 in 3rd C.

to finish

Sew across the bottom of the bag. Sew
the two handles to the inside of the bag
approximately 8 cm (3 in) from outside edge.
Sew in any loose ends.

Put the bag into the washing machine at
60°C to felt it (see page 24).

When the bag is dry sew the flowers to it,
following photograph for positions. Sew the
beads randomly all over the top section of
the bag, in the centres of the flowers and
around the edges of the handles.

Fold the rectangle of lining fabric in half and,
taking 2 cm (¾ in) turnings, machine stitch
the two long sides together. Press under
2 cm (¾ in) around the top edge. WS facing,
slip the lining into the bag and sew the
pressed edge to the first row of the top of
the bag.

Beaded evening bag

Simple embroidery and beading give this little felted clutch bag glamour: make it in colours to match your favourite party dress.

Size
Approximately 29 x 16 cm (11½ x 6¼ in) after washing

Materials
Scottish Tweed DK
2 50 g balls in Main Shade (**MS**) purple/Thistle 16
1 50 g ball in 1st Contrast (**1st C**) lavender/Lavender 5
3.50 mm (UK 9) crochet hook
Tapestry needle
Beads in a contrast colour
Beading needle and thread
2 40-cm (16-in) long pieces of 2.5-cm (1-in) wide plum ribbon
Sewing thread to match ribbon
Sewing needle

Tension
18 sts and 12 rows to 10 cm (4 in) over treble fabric BEFORE WASHING on 3.50 mm (UK 9) crochet hook or the size required to achieve this tension.

Abbreviations
1st C 1st Contrast
beg beginning
ch chain
cm centimetres
cont continue
in inches
mm millimetres
rem remain(ing)
MS Main Shade
rep repeat
st(s) stitch(es)
tr treble
tr2tog work 2 tr into ch sp until 1 loop of each remains on hook, yarn over hook and through all 3 loops on hook
WS wrong side

Front

With 3.50 mm (UK 9) crochet hook and MS make 60 ch.

1st row: 1 tr into 4th ch from hook, 1 tr into each ch to end, turn. 58 sts.

2nd row: 3 ch (counts as first tr), miss first tr, 1 tr into each tr, 1 tr into 3rd of 3 ch, turn.

Rep last row until work measures 18 cm (7 in).

Fasten off.

Back

With 3.50 mm (UK 9) crochet hook and MS make 60 ch.

Work as for front until work measures 18 cm (7 in).

Front flap

Next row: 3 ch (counts as first tr), miss first tr, tr2tog over next 2 tr, 1 tr into each tr to last 3 sts, tr2tog over next 2 tr, 1 tr into 3rd of 3 ch, turn.

Rep last row 7 more times.

Fasten off.

to finish

Sew in any loose ends.

Felt the bag pieces (see page 24). When both pieces are dry place them WS facing and neatly sew them together along the sides and bottom.

Using 1st C embroider the bag, following the photograph. Using beads, highlight the embroidery.

Sew a length of ribbon to the inside edge of the front flap and a length to the front of the bag for fastening.

Square shoulder bag

Cool colours and retro style make this shoulder bag
a must-have for all fashion-conscious crochet fans.
It is surprisingly simple to make, too!

Size
32 x 32 cm (12½ x 12½ in) excluding handle

Materials
Rowan Summer Tweed
2 50 g hanks in Main Shade (**MS**) pale brown/Raffia 515
2 50 g hanks in 1st Contrast (**1st C**) pale green/Rush 507
2 50 g hanks in 2nd Contrast (**2nd C**) pale grey/Ghost 506
2 50 g hanks in 3rd Contrast (**3rd C**) ecru/Oats 508
4.00 mm (UK 8) crochet hook
Tapestry needle
Rowan buckle code 00367

Tension
Each square measures 8 x 8 cm (3 x 3 in)

Abbreviations
1st C 1st Contrast
2nd C 2nd Contrast
3rd C 3rd Contrast
beg beginning
ch chain
cm centimetres
cont continue
in inches
mm millimetres
MS Main Shade
rep repeat
sp space
ss slip stitch
st(s) stitch(es)
tr treble

Basic square (make 55)

With 4.00 mm (UK 8) crochet hook and MS make 6 ch, ss into first ch to form a ring.

1st round: 3 ch (counts as first tr), 15 tr into ring, ss into 3rd of 3 ch.
Change to 1st C.

2nd round: 3 ch (counts as first tr), 2 tr into same st as ss, 2 ch, miss 1 tr, 1 tr into next tr, 2 ch, miss 1 tr, *3 tr into next tr, 2 ch, miss 1 tr, 1 tr into next tr, 2 ch, miss 1 tr, rep from * twice more, ss into 3rd of 3 ch.
Change to 2nd C.

3rd round: 3 ch (counts as first tr), *5 tr into next tr, 1 tr into next tr, 2 tr into next ch sp, 1 tr into next tr, 2 tr into next ch sp, 1 tr into next tr, rep from twice more, 5 tr into next tr, 1 tr into next tr, 2 tr into next ch sp, 1 tr into next tr, 2 tr into next ch sp, ss into top of 3 ch.
Fasten off.

Use this basic square pattern to make all 55 squares, but change the colours on each square making sure you use all 4 colours randomly.

Buckle carrier

With 4.00 mm (UK 8) crochet hook and MS make 11 ch.

1st row: 1 tr into 4th ch from hook, 1 tr into each ch to end, turn. 9 sts.

2nd row: 3 ch (counts as first tr), 1 tr into each tr, 1 tr into 3rd of 3 ch, turn.
Rep 2nd row until work measures 14 cm (5½ in).
Fasten off.

Fastening strap

Work as for buckle carrier but cont until work measures 27 cm (10½ in).
Fasten off.

to finish

Sew in any loose ends.

Using a random selection of squares, sew together 16 squares for the front (4 squares wide by 4 squares long) and the same for the back.

Sew together a strip of 4 squares for each side and the bottom of the bag and sew to the front and back.

Sew 11 squares together for the strap and sew the ends of the strap to the top of each side of the bag.

Fold the buckle carrier in half around the central buckle bar (making sure the buckle is the right way up with the silver end facing upwards) and sew the ends to the front of the bag approximately 19 cm (7½ in) down from the top edge, following the photograph. Sew one end of the fastening strap to the inside of the bag at the top centre of the back. With 4.00 mm (UK 8) crochet hook and MS make 14 ch, leaving lengths of yarn at each end. Thread the tapestry needle with the yarn at one end and sew it to the edge of the buckle carrier, approximately halfway down. Sew the other end to the opposite edge of the carrier to make a loop to tuck the end of the fastening strap into when the bag is closed.

Beaded make-up bag

This attractive but practical make-up bag with beaded detailing will hold all your essential make-up items and look great at the same time.

Size
14 x 17 cm (5½ x 6¾ in)

Materials
Rowan 4-ply Soft
1 50 g ball in Main Shade (**MS**) pale green/Folly 391
1 50 g ball in 1st Contrast (**1st C**) green/Leafy 367
1 50 g ball in 2nd Contrast (**2nd C**) blue/Blue Bird 369
3.00 mm (UK 11) crochet hook
Tapestry needle
Zip
Small beads in contrast colour
Beading needle and thread

Tension
26 sts and 32 rows to 10 cm (4 in) measured over double crochet on 3.00 mm (UK 11) crochet hook or size required to achieve this tension.

Abbreviations
1st C 1st Contrast
2nd C 2nd Contrast
ch chain
cm centimetres
cont continue
dc double crochet
in inches
mm millimetres
MS Main Shade
rep repeat
sp space
tr treble

Bag (worked in 1 piece)

With 3.00 mm (UK 11) crochet hook and MS make 90 ch.

1st row: 1 ch (does not count as first dc), 1 dc into first ch, 1 dc into each ch to end, turn. 90 dc.

2nd row: 1 ch, 1 dc into first dc, 1 dc into each dc to end, turn.

Rep 2nd row twice more.

Change to 1st C.

Work 4 rows as 2nd row.

Change to 2nd C.

Work 4 rows as 2nd row.

These 12 rows form the colour stripe rep. Cont working 12-row stripe rep until work measures 14 cm (5½ in) finishing with a full 4-row colour rep.

Fasten off.

Frill (make one in each colour)

With 3.00 mm (UK 11) crochet hook and MS make 92 ch.

1st row (RS): 1 dc into 2nd ch from hook, 1 dc into each ch to end, turn. 91 dc.

2nd row: 3 ch (counts as first tr), miss first dc, 1 tr into each of next 3 dc, *3 ch, miss 3 dc, 1 tr into each of next 7 dc, rep from * to end omitting 3 tr at end of last rep, turn.

3rd row: 1 ch, 1 dc into each of next 4 tr, 3 dc into next 3 ch sp, *1 dc into each of next 7 tr, 3 dc into next 3 ch sp, rep from * to last 4 tr, 1 dc into each of next 3 tr, 1 dc into 3rd of 3 ch, turn.

4th row: 1 ch, 1 dc into first dc, 2 ch, miss 2 dc, 1 dc into next dc, 8 ch, miss 3 dc, 1 dc into next dc, *5 ch, miss 5 dc, 1 dc into next dc, 8ch, miss 3 dc, 1 dc into next dc, rep from * to last 3 dc, 2 ch, 1 dc into last dc, turn.

5th row: 1 ch, 1 dc into first dc, 19 tr into 8 ch arch, *1 dc into next 5 ch sp, 19 tr into next 8 ch arch, rep from * to last 2 ch sp, 1 dc into last dc.

Fasten off.

to finish

Sew in any loose ends.
Sew down the back seam and across the
bottom of the bag. Sew the zip into the top of
the bag.
Sew first frill 1 colour repeat down from top
of the bag, the next frill just underneath the
first one and the third just underneath the
second one. Sew a strand of 6 beads
between each arch on each coloured frill.

Floral bag

Embellished with beaded flowers and leaves, this shapely bag will attract attention wherever you take it, whether it's to the office or an evening out.

Size
34 x 31 cm (13¼ x 12¼ in) excluding handle

Materials
Rowan Felted Tweed
8 50 g balls in Main Shade (**MS**) pink/Melody 142
1 50 g ball in 1st Contrast (**1st C**) red/Rage 150
1 50 g ball in 2nd Contrast (**2nd C**) purple/Treacle 145
1 50 g ball in 3rd Contrast (**3rd C**) green/Herb 146
1 50 g ball in 4th Contrast (**4th C**) blue/Watery 152
5.00 mm (UK 6) crochet hook.
3.00 mm (UK 11) crochet hook
Tapestry needle
Purchased handle
Beads to match yarns
Beading needle and thread

Tension
15 sts and 19 rows to 10 cm (4 in) measured over double crochet using 2 ends of yarn on 5.00 mm (UK 6) crochet hook or the size required to achieve this tension.

Abbreviations
1st C 1st Contrast
2nd C 2nd Contrast
3rd C 3rd Contrast
4th C 4th Contrast
beg beginning
ch chain
cm centimetres
cont continue
dc double crochet
dc2tog [insert hook into next dc, yarn over hook and draw loop through] twice, yarn over hook and through all 3 loops on hook
dtr double treble
folls follows
htr half treble
in inches
mm millimetres
MS Main Shade
rem remain
rep repeat
RS right side
ss slip stitch
tr2tog 1 tr into each of next 2 dc until 1 loop of each remains on hook, yarn over and through all 3 loops on hook
tr treble

(Please note that 1 ch at beg of rows does not count as first st.)

Bag (make 2)

With 5.00 mm (UK 6) crochet hook and 2 ends of MS make 54 ch.

1st row: 1 dc into 2nd ch from hook, 1 dc into each ch to end, turn. 53 dc.

2nd row: 1 ch, dc2tog into first 2 dc, dc to last 2 dc, dc2tog, turn.

3rd row: 1 ch, 1 dc into each dc to end, turn.

4th row: As 2nd row.

5th row: As 3rd row.

6th row: As 2nd row.

7th, 8th and 9th rows: As 3rd row.

10th row: As 2nd row.

Rep rows 7–10 until 27 sts rem.

Cont straight until work measures 31 cm (12¼ in).

Fasten off.

Large flower

With 3.00 mm (UK 11) crochet hook and 1st C make 7 ch, ss into first ch to form a ring.

1st round: 1 ch, 16 dc into ring, ss into first dc.

2nd round: 1 ch, 1 dc into first dc, (5 ch, miss 1 dc, 1 dc into next dc) 7 times, 5 ch, ss into first dc.

3rd round: ss into first 5 ch arch, 1 ch, (1 dc, 5 htr, 1 dc) into each 5 ch arch, ss into first dc. (8 petals)

4th round: 1 ch, working behind each petal work 1 dc into first dc on 2nd round, (6 ch, 1 dc into next dc on 2nd round) 7 times, 6 ch, ss into first dc.

5th round: ss into first 6 ch arch, 1 ch, (1 dc, 6 htr, 1 dc) into each 6 ch arch to end, ss into first dc.

Fasten off.

Make 2 more flowers in the same way using 2nd C.

Small flower

With 3.00 mm (UK 11) crochet hook and 1st C make 6 ch, ss into first ch to form a ring.

1st round: 1 ch, 15 dc into ring, ss into first dc.

2nd round: (3 ch, tr2tog over next 2 dc, 3 ch, ss into next dc) 5 times placing last ss into last dc of previous round. Fasten off.

Make another 2 flowers in same way in 1st C and 5 flowers in 2nd C.

Large leaf

With 3.00 mm (UK 11) crochet hook and 3rd C make 15 ch and work as folls: 1 dc into 2nd ch from hook, working 1 st into each ch work 1 htr, 3 tr, 4 dtr, 3 tr, 1 htr and 1 dc, 3 ch, then working 1 st into each ch on other side of ch work 1 dc, 1 htr, 3 tr, 4 dtr, 3 tr, 1 htr, 1 dc, ss into first dc.

Fasten off.

Make 5 more leaves.

Small leaf

With 3.00 mm (UK 11) crochet hook and 4th C make 9 ch and work as folls: 1 dc into 2nd ch from hook, working 1 st into each ch work, 1 htr, 4 tr, 1 htr, 1 dc, and 3 ch, then working 1 st into each ch on other side of ch work, 1 dc, 1 htr, 4 tr, 1 htr, 1 dc, ss into first dc.

Fasten off.

Make 4 more leaves.

Tabs (make 4)

With 5.00 mm (UK 6) crochet hook and 2 ends of MS make 6 ch.

1st row: 1 dc into 2nd ch from hook, 1 dc into each ch to end, turn. 5 dc.

2nd row: 1 ch, 1 dc into first dc, 1 dc into each dc to end, turn.

Rep last row until work measures 9 cm (3½ in).

Fasten off.

to finish

RS of bag facing, sew up approximately 20 cm (8 in) of each side of the bag leaving the sides open near the top. Sew across the bottom of the bag. Fold the tabs in half through the carriers on the handles and sew the ends to the top front and back of the bag, following the photograph.

Sew the flowers and leaves to the bag following the photograph. Embellish the flowers and leaves with beads, sewing them on to best effect.

Sew in any loose ends.

If you wish you can make flowers and leaves for the other side of the bag.

hats, mittens & more

Cool key ring

Wonderfully funky and lots of fun, this fantastic key ring will make it near impossible for you to ever mislay your keys again.

Size
16 cm (6¼ in) in length (including finding), star measures 5.5 cm (2¼ in) across; balls measure 2 cm (¾ in) wide

Materials
Rowan 4-ply Cotton
1 50 g ball in Main Shade (**MS**) lime/Fresh 131
Scottish Tweed 4-ply
1 25 g ball in 1st Contrast (**1st C**) pale green/Machair 02
RYC Cashcotton DK
1 50 g ball in 2nd Contrast (**2nd C**) pale aqua/Pool 602
2.50 mm (UK 12) crochet hook
Tapestry needle
Beads in contrast colours
Beading needle and thread
Key ring finding

Tension
It is difficult to specify a tension on this pattern so simply work to the measurements given.

Abbreviations
1st C 1st Contrast
2nd C 2nd Contrast
ch chain
cm centimetres
dc double crochet
dc2tog [insert hook in next st, yarn over hook and draw loop through] twice, yarn over hook and draw through all 3 loops
htr half treble
in inches
mm millimetres
MS Main Shade
rep repeat
sp spaces
ss slip stitch
st(s) stitch(es)
tr treble
WS wrong side

Star (make 2)

With 2.50 mm (UK 12) crochet hook and MS make 6 ch, ss into first ch to form a ring.

1st round (RS): 1 ch, 18 dc into ring, ss into first dc.

2nd round: 9 ch, 1 dc into 4th ch from hook, 1 htr into each of next 2 ch, 1 tr into each of next 3 ch, miss first 3 dc on ring, ss into next dc, *9 ch, 1 dc into 4th ch from hook, 1 htr into each of next 2 ch, 1 tr into each of next 3 ch, miss next 2 dc on ring, ss into next dc, rep from * 4 more times, with last ss into same st as ss of previous round.
Fasten off.

Large ball

With 2.50 mm (UK 12) crochet hook and MS make 3 ch, ss into first ch.

1st round: 1 ch, 2 dc into each ch to end, ss into first dc. (6 dc)

2nd round: 1 ch, 2 dc into each dc to end, ss into first dc. (12 dc)

3rd round: 1 ch, 1 dc into each dc to end, ss into first dc.
Rep 3rd round until work measures 3 cm (1¼ in).

Next round: 1 ch, (dc2tog) 6 times, ss into first dc. (6 sts)
Stuff the ball before closing the hole up.

Next round: 1 ch, (dc2tog) 3 times, ss into first dc. (3 sts)
Fasten off and pull 3 sts together to close the hole.

Small ball

Work as for large ball but make the ball 2 cm (¾ in) in length.

Curls

With 2.50 mm (UK 12) crochet hook and 2nd C make 24 ch.

1st row: 1 dc into 2nd ch from hook, 1 dc into ch to end.
Fasten off.
Make 1 more curl using 2nd C and 2 curls using 1st C.

Key cover

With 2.50 mm (UK 12) crochet hook and 1st C make 4 ch, ss into first ch.

1st round: 1 ch, 1 dc into each ch to end, ss into first dc. (4 dc)

2nd round: 1 ch, 2 dc into each dc to end, ss into first dc. (8 dc)

3rd round: 1 ch, 1 dc into each dc to end, ss into first dc.

4th round: 1 ch, 2 dc into each dc to end, ss into first dc. (16 dc)

5th round: 1 ch, 1 dc into each dc to end, ss into first dc.
Rep 5th round 4 more times.
Fasten off.

to finish

Sew in any loose ends.

WS facing, sew the star pieces together around all the edges. Sew a row of beads around the edges on both sides. Make a 9 cm (3½ in) length of ch using MS and attach one end to the star and the other inside the key cover.

Make a small pompom (see page 22) in 2nd C. Make a 7 cm (2¾ in) length of ch using 2nd C and attach one end to the pompom and the other end to the inside of the key cover.

Make a small pompom in 1st C. Make a 4 cm (1½ in) length of ch using 1st C and attach one end to the pompom and the other end to the inside of the key cover.

Attach three strands of beads, each 11 beads long, to the small ball. Make a 8 cm (3 in) length of ch using MS and attach one end to the top of the ball and the other end to the inside of the key cover.

Randomly sew contrast colour beads all over the large ball. Make a 5 cm (2 in) length of ch using MS and attach one end to the top of the ball and the other end to the inside of the key cover.

Next, attach all 4 curls to the inside of the key cover.

Randomly sew contrast colour beads all over the key cover.

Finally, sew the key ring finding to the top of the key cover.

Flower beanie

This cute hat with its beaded flower uses basic stitches to stunning effect. It's so simple to make that you'll end up with one to match every outfit.

Size
To fit average adult size head

Materials
Rowan Kid Classic

• Colourway 1
1 50 g ball in Main Shade (**MS**) lilac/Frilly 844
1 50 g ball in 1st Contrast (**1st C**) purple/Royal 835
4.50 mm (UK 7) crochet hook
Tapestry needle
Beads in complementary colours for centre of flowers
Beading needle and thread

• Colourway 2
1 50 g ball in Main Shade (**MS**) cream/Feather 828
1 50 g ball in 1st Contrast (**1st C**) pale blue/Glacier 822
4.50 mm (UK 7) crochet hook.
Tapestry needle
Beads in complementary colours for centre of flowers
Beading needle and thread

Tension
19 sts and 10 rows to 10 cm (4 in) measured over pattern of 6th and 7th rounds on 4.50 mm (UK 7) crochet hook or size to achieve this tension.

Abbreviations
1st C 1st Contrast
beg beginning
ch chain
cm centimetres
dc double crochet
dtr double treble
in inches
mm millimetres
MS Main Shade
rep repeat
sp spaces
ss slip stitch
st(s) stitch(es)
tr treble

Beanie

With a 4.50 mm (UK 7) crochet hook and MS make 96 ch, ss into first ch to form a ring.

1st round: 1 ch, 1 dc into each ch to end, ss into first dc.

2nd round: 1 ch, 1 dc into each dc to end, ss into first dc. 96 dc.

Rep last round twice more.

5th round: 3 ch (counts as first tr), 1 tr into each of next 2 dc, *1 ch, miss 1 dc, 1 tr into each of next 3 dc, rep from * to last st, 1 ch, miss 1 st, ss into top of 3 ch.

6th round: 4 ch (counts as 1 tr, 1 ch), miss 1 tr, 1 tr into next tr, 1 tr into 1 ch sp, 1 tr into next tr, *1 ch, miss 1 tr, 1 tr into next tr, 1 tr into next ch sp, 1 tr into next tr, rep from * to last 3 sts, 1 ch, miss 1 tr, 1 tr into next tr, 1 tr into next ch sp, ss into 3rd of 4th ch.

7th round: 3 ch (counts as first tr), *1 tr into next ch sp, 1 tr into next tr, 1 ch, miss 1 tr, 1 tr into next tr, rep from * to last 3 sts, 1 tr into ch sp, 1 tr into next tr, 1 ch, miss 1 tr, ss into 3rd of 3 ch at beg of round.

Rep 6th and 7th rounds 3 more times.

14th round: 4 ch (counts as first tr, 1 ch), miss 1 tr, 1 tr into next tr, *miss 1 ch sp, 1 tr into next tr, 1 ch, miss 1 tr, 1 tr into next tr, rep from * to end, ss into 3rd of 3 ch.

15th round: 3 ch (counts as first tr), *1 tr into next ch sp, 1 ch, miss 1 tr, 1 tr into next tr, rep from * to last 2 sts, 1 tr into next ch sp, 1 ch, miss 1 tr, ss into 3rd of 3 ch.

16th round: 4 ch (counts as 1 tr, 1 ch), *miss 1 tr, 1 tr into next ch sp, 1 tr into next tr, 1 ch, rep from * to last 2 sts, miss 1 tr, 1 tr into next ch sp, ss into 3rd of 3 ch.

17th round: ss into first ch sp, 3 ch (counts as first tr), 1 tr into each ch sp to end, ss into 3rd of 3 ch.

18th round: 3 ch (counts as first tr), 1 tr into sp after each tr to end, ss into 3rd of 3 ch.

19th round: 3 ch (counts as first tr), miss 1 tr, *1 tr into sp after missed tr, miss 2 tr, rep from * to end, ss into 3rd of 3 ch.

Rep last round once more.

Fasten off, thread end through top of each st, draw up and secure.

Edging

With 4.50 mm (UK 7) crochet hook join 1st C to lower edge, 1 ch, 1 dc into each ch, ss to first dc. Fasten off.

Flower

With 4.50 mm (UK 7) crochet hook and 1st C make 5 ch, ss into first ch to form a ring. Flower can be worked in 1st C only or change to MS for rounds 2 and 3.

1st round: 1 ch, work 10 dc into ring, ss into first dc.

2nd round: 1 ch, work 1 dc into each dc, ss into first dc.

3rd round: 2 ch (counts as 1 htr), miss first dc, work 2 htr into each of next 9 dc, 1 htr into first dc, ss into 2nd of 2 ch. 20 sts.

4th round: *2 ch, working into front loop only of each htr work 2 tr into each of next 3 htr, 2 ch, ss into next htr, rep from * 4 more times placing last ss into 2nd of 2 ch at beg of previous round. (5 petals)

5th round: Working behind each petal of previous round and into back loop of each htr on 3rd round, *4 ch, work 2 dtr into each of next 3 htr, 4 ch, ss into next htr, rep from * 4 more times placing last ss into same place as ss at end of round 5.

Fasten off.

to finish

Sew in any loose ends.

Sew beads to the centre of the flower, following the photograph. Sew the flower onto one side of the hat just above the band.

Stripy hat

With earflaps for extra warmth, this hat will keep out the cold and keep you looking cool. Matching stripy mittens (see page 104) complete the look.

Size
To fit average size adult head

Materials
Rowan Wool Cotton
2 50 g balls in Main Shade (**MS**) blue/August 953
2 50 g balls in 1st Contrast (**1st C**) pale blue/Violet 933
4.00 mm (UK 8) crochet hook
Tapestry needle

Tension
19 sts and 24 rows to 10 cm (4 in) measured over double crochet on 4.00 mm (UK 8) crochet hook or the size required to achieve this tension.

Abbreviations
1st C 1st Contrast
beg beginning
ch chain
cluster work 3 tr into next st but leave the last loop of each tr on the hook, yarn over and draw through all 4 loops
cm centimetres
cont continue
dc double crochet
dc2tog [insert hook into next st, yarn over hook and draw loop through] twice, yarn over hook and draw through all 3 loops
dec decrease
in inches
mm millimetres
MS Main Shade
rem remain
rep repeat
sp space
ss slip stitch
st(s) stitch(es)
tr treble
tr2tog work 2 tr into next st until 1 loop of each remains on hook, yarn over hook and through all 3 loops on hook

(Please note that 1 ch at beg of a round does not count as first st.)

Hat

With 4.00 mm (UK 8) crochet hook and MS make 92 ch, join with a ss to form a ring.

1st round: 1 ch, 1 dc into each ch to end, ss into first dc.

2nd round: 1 ch, 1 dc into each dc to end, ss into first dc.

Change to 1st C.

3rd round: As 2nd round.

4th round: As 2nd round.

Change to MS.

5th to 12th rounds: As 2nd round changing colour every 2 rounds.

Change to MS.

13th round: 3 ch (counts as first tr), 1 tr into each of next 2 dc, *miss 1 dc, 2 ch, 1 tr into each of next 3 dc, rep from * to last dc, miss 1 dc, 2 ch, ss into 3rd of 3 ch.

Change to 1st C.

14th round: ss into first tr, 3 ch (counts as 1st tr), tr2tog into first tr, 3 ch, 3 tr cluster into same tr, *miss (1 tr, 2 ch, 1tr) (1 cluster, 3 ch, 1 cluster) into next tr, rep from * to end, ss into 3rd of 3 ch.

Change to MS.

15th round: 3 ch (counts as first tr) 3 tr into 3 ch sp, *1 ch, 3 tr into next ch sp, rep from * to last st, 1 ch, ss into 3rd of 3 ch.

Change to 1st C.

16th round: 1 ch, 1 dc into each st to end, ss into first dc. 93 dc.

17th round: 1 ch, 1 dc into each dc to end, ss into first dc.

Change to MS.

18th round: 1 ch, (9 dc, dc2tog) to last 5 sts, 1 dc into each of last 5 sts, ss into first dc. (85 sts)

19th round: 1 ch, 1 dc into each dc to end, ss into first dc.

Change to 1st C.

20th round: 1 ch, (8 dc, dc2tog) to last 5 sts, 1 dc into each of last 5 sts, ss into first dc. (77 sts)

21st round: 1 ch, 1 dc into each dc to end, ss into first dc.
Change to MS.
22nd round: 1 ch, (7 dc, dc2tog) to last 5 dc, 1 dc into each of last 5 dc, ss into first dc. (69 sts)
23rd round: 1 ch, 1 dc into each dc to end, ss into first dc.
Change to 1st C.
24th round: 1 ch, (6dc, dc2tog) to last 5 dc, 1 dc into each of last 5 dc, ss into first dc. (61 sts)
25th round: 1 ch, 1 dc into each dc to end, ss into first dc.
Change to MS.
26th round: 1 ch, (5 dc, dc2tog) to last 5 sts, 1 dc into each of last 5 sts, ss into first dc. (53 sts)
27th round: 1 ch, 1 dc into each dc to end, ss into first dc.
Change to 1st C.
28th round: 1 ch, (4 dc, dc2tog) to last 5 sts, 1 dc into each of last 5 sts, ss into first dc. (45 sts)
29th round: 1 ch, 1 dc into each dc to end.
Change to MS.
30th round: 1 ch, (3 dc, dc2tog) to last 5 sts, 1 dc into each of last 5 sts, ss into first dc. (37 sts)
31st round: 1 ch, 1 dc into each dc to end, ss into first dc.
Change to 1st C.
32nd round: 1 ch, (2 dc, dc2tog) to last 5 sts, 1 dc into each of last 5 sts, ss into first dc. (29 sts)
33rd round: 1 ch, (1 dc, dc2tog) to last 2 sts, 1 dc into each of last 2 sts, ss into first dc. (20 sts)
Change to MS.
34th round: 1 ch, (1 dc, dc2tog) to last 2 sts, 1 dc into each of last 2 dc, ss into first dc. (14 sts)
35th round: 1 ch, (dc2tog) to end, ss into first dc. (7 sts)
Fasten off by threading end through last 7 sts and drawing up.

Ear flaps

Working into other side of foundation ch join 1st C in 11th ch after centre back seam.
Using 4.00 mm (UK 8) crochet hook and 1st C work as folls:
1st row: 1 dc into each of next 22 ch of foundation row, turn.
2nd row: 1 ch, 1 dc into each dc to end, turn.
Change to MS.
3rd row: 1 ch, 1 dc into first dc, dc2tog over next 2 dc, 1 dc into each dc to last 3 dc, dc2tog into next dc, 1 dc into last dc, turn.
4th row: 1 ch, 1 dc into each dc to end, turn.
Change to 1st C.
5th row: As 3rd row.
6th row: As 4th row.
7th row: As 3rd row.
8th row: As 4th row.
Change to 1st C.
Cont to dec 1 st at each end of next and every alternate row and changing colour every 2 rows until 4 sts rem.
9th row: 1 ch, (dc2tog) twice, turn.
10th row: 1 ch, dc2tog.
Fasten off.
Joining 1st C to 32nd ch to right of centre back seam, work the other ear flap to match.

to finish

Sew in any loose ends.

With 4.00 mm (UK 8) crochet hook and 1st C work 1 round of dc around all edges of the hat and ear flaps working dc2tog at the inner corners of the ear flaps. Change to MS. Work another row of dc around all edges of the hat. Fasten off.

Make a pompom (see page 22) using both yarns and sew it to the top of the hat.

Plaits (make 2)

With 4.00 mm (UK 8) crochet hook and MS make 30 ch, leaving a length of yarn at each end to attach. Make 2 more in MS and 3 in 1st C.

Plait all 6 strands together taking one length of each colour into each group. Knot one end and sew the other end to the point of an ear flap. Unravel the ends of yarn below the knot.

Stripy mittens

These cute lace-top mittens will match your stripy hat (see page 98) and keep your fingers toasty. A piping mug of hot chocolate will give extra warmth.

Size
To fit average size adult hands

Materials
Rowan Wool Cotton
2 50 g balls in Main Shade(**MS**) blue/August 953
2 50 g balls in 1st Contrast (**1st C**) pale blue/Violet 933
4.00 mm (UK 8) crochet hook
Tapestry needle

Tension
19 sts and 24 rows to 10 cm (4 in) measured over double crochet on 4.00 mm (UK 8) crochet hook or size required to achieve this tension.

Abbreviations
1st C 1st Contrast
beg beginning
ch chain
cm centimetres
cont continue
dc double crochet
in inches
mm millimetres
MS Main Shade
rem remain(ing)
rep repeat
RS right side
sp space
ss slip stitch
st(s) stitch(es)
tr treble

(Please note that 1 ch at beg of any row does not count as first st throughout pattern.)

Back of mitten (make 2)

With 4.00 mm (UK 8) crochet hook and MS make 11 ch.

1st row: 1 dc into 2nd ch from hook, 1 dc into each ch to end, turn. (10 dc)

2nd row: 1 ch, 2 dc into first dc, 1 dc into each dc to last st, 2 dc into last dc, turn. (12 dc)

Change to 1st C.

3rd row: 1 ch, 1 dc into each dc to end, turn.

4th row: As 2nd row. (14 dc)

Change to MS.

5th row: As 3rd row.

6th row: As 2nd row. (16 dc)

Cont increasing and changing colour on every 2nd row until there are 22 dc.

Cont straight in stripe pattern until work measures 17 cm (6¾ in) ending with 2 rows of MS.

Change to 1st C.

Next row: 1 ch, *2 dc into next dc, 1 dc into each of next 2 dc, rep from * to last st, 2 dc into last dc, turn. (30 dc)

Next row: 1 ch, 1 dc into each dc to end, turn.

Lace top of mitten

1st row: 3 ch (counts as first tr), 1 tr into next dc, *miss 2 dc, into next dc work (3 tr, 1 ch, 3 tr), miss 2 dc, 1 tr into each of next 2 dc, rep from * to end, turn.

2nd row: 3 ch (counts as first tr), 1 tr into next tr, *miss 3 tr, into next 1 ch sp work (3 tr, 1 ch, 3 tr), miss 3 tr, 1 tr into each of next 2 tr, rep from * to end, working last tr into 3rd of 3 ch, turn.

Rep 2nd row twice more.

Fasten off.

Palm of mitten (make 2)

With 4.00 mm (UK 8) crochet hook and MS make 9 ch.

1st row: 1 dc into 2nd ch from hook, 1 dc into each ch to end, turn. (8 dc)

2nd row: 1 ch, 2 dc into first dc, 1 dc into each dc to last dc, 2 dc into last dc, turn. Change to 1st C. (10 dc)

3rd row: 1 ch, 1 dc into each dc to end, turn.

4th row: As 2nd row. (12 dc)

Change to MS.

5th row: As 3rd row.

6th row: As 2nd row. (14 dc)

Cont increasing and changing colour on every 2nd row until there are 16 sts.

Cont straight in stripe pattern until work measures 17 cm (6¾ in) ending with 2 rows of MS.

Change to 1st C.

Next row: 1 ch, *2 dc into first dc, 1 dc into each of next 2 dc, rep from * to last 4 sts, 2 dc into next dc, 1 dc into next dc, 2 dc into each of next 2 dc, turn. (23 dc)

Next row: 1 ch, 1 dc into each dc to end, turn.

Work lace top as back of mitten.

Fasten off.

Thumb (make 2)

With 4.00 mm (UK 8) crochet hook and MS make 4 ch, ss into first ch to form a ring.

1st round: 1 ch, 8 dc into ring, ss into first dc.

2nd round: 1 ch, *2 dc into first dc, 1 dc into next dc, rep from * to end, ss into first dc. (12 sts)

Change to 1st C.

3rd round: 1 ch, 1 dc into each dc to end, ss into first dc.

4th round: As 3rd round.

Change to MS.

Cont working 3rd round, changing colour every 2nd round, until work measures 6.5 cm (2⅝ in) or length required for your thumb.

Fasten off.

to finish

Sew in any loose ends.

RS facing, place the back of a mitten on the palm of a mitten and sew down one side. Starting at lace edge, sew approximately 11 cm (4½ in) up the other side. Insert the thumb and sew around the thumb edge. Sew remainder of the side across the bottom of the mitten.

Sew the other mitten together, reversing the thumb side so you have left and right mittens. Turn the mittens RS out.

With MS make a length of ch approximately 50 cm (20 in) long. Thread it through the top of the last row of dc, starting at the centre back of mitten and working around. Make 4 small pompoms (see page 22) and attach them to the lengths of ch, following the photograph. Tie the ends into a bow.

Elegant choker

This elegant, sophisticated choker looks so good that no one will ever guess how easy it is to make. It's a perfect accessory for a graceful evening dress.

Size
To fit an average size neck

Materials
Rowan 4-ply Soft
1 50 g ball in wine/Victoria 390
3.00 mm (UK 11) crochet hook
Tapestry needle
Small beads in contrast colour
4 large beads in toning colour
Beading needle and thread

Tension
26 sts and 32 rows to 10 cm (4 in) measured over double crochet worked with a 3.00 mm (UK 11) crochet hook or size required to achieve this tension.

Abbreviations
beg beginning
ch chain
cm centimetres
dc double crochet
htr half treble
in inches
mm millimetres
rep repeat
ss slip stitch
st(s) stitch(es)

Choker

With 3.00 mm (UK 11) crochet hook make
68 ch.
1st row: 1 dc into 2nd ch from hook, 1 dc into
each ch to end, turn. (67 dc)
2nd row: 1 ch (does not count as first dc),
1 dc into first dc, 1 dc into each dc to end,
turn.
Rep 2nd row until work measures 2¼ cm
(⅞ in).
Fasten off.

Ties (make 4)

With 3.00 mm (UK 11) crochet hook make
90 ch leaving lengths of yarn at each end for
attaching to choker.

Small flower

With 3.00 mm (UK 11) crochet hook make
6 ch, ss into first ch to form a ring.
1st round: 1 ch, (1 dc, 8 ch) 10 times into
ring, ss into first dc.
Fasten off.

Medium flower

With 3.00 mm (UK 11) crochet hook make
5 ch, ss into first ch to form a ring.
1st round: 1 ch, 10 dc into ring, ss into first
dc.
2nd round: 1 ch, 1 dc into each dc, ss into
first dc.
3rd round: 2 ch (counts as 1htr), miss first
dc, work 2 htr into each of next 9 dc, 1 htr into
first dc, ss into 2nd of 2 ch. (20 sts)
4th round: *2 ch, 2 tr into each of next 3 htr,
2 ch, ss into next htr, rep from * 4 more times
placing last ss into 2nd of 2 ch at beg of
previous round. (5 petals)
Fasten off.

Large flower

With 3.00 mm (UK 11) crochet hook make
6 ch, ss into first ch to form a ring.
1st round: 1 ch, (1 dc, 18 ch) 5 times into
ring, ss into first dc.
Fasten off.

to finish

Sew in any loose ends.
Sew the small flower into middle of the
medium flower and the large flower to the
back of the medium flower, making sure that
each loop of the large flower is sewn to a
corner of each petal on the medium flower.
Sew the flower to the middle of the choker.
Sew a tie to each corner of choker. Sew
small beads to the flower, following the
photograph, and large beads to the ends
of ties.

Delicate necklace

It takes just a little time to make this pretty, unique necklace that'll add a touch of glitz and glamour to any outfit on an evening out.

Size
Approximately 58 cm (23 in) long; flowers measure 2.5 cm (1 in) across

Materials
Rowan Lurex Shimmer
1 25 g ball in Main Shade (**MS**) pale gold/Antique White Gold 332
1 25 g ball in 1st Contrast (**1st C**) copper/Copper 330
1 25 g ball in 2nd Contrast (**2nd C**) bronze/Bronze 335
2.00 mm (UK 14) crochet hook
Tapestry needle

Tension
It is difficult to specify a tension on this pattern so simply work to the measurements given.

Abbreviations
1st C 1st Contrast
2nd C 2nd Contrast
ch chain
cm centimetres
dc double crochet
in inches
mm millimetres
MS Main Shade
ss slip stitch
tr2tog 1 tr into each of next 2 dc until 1 loop of each remains on hook, yarn over hook and through all 3 loops on hook

Necklace (make 4 in MS, 3 in 1st C and 3 in 2nd C)

With 2.00 mm (UK 14) crochet hook and make 100 cm (39 in) of chain st leaving lengths of yarn at each end to sew to tassel.

Flower (make 3 in each colour)

With 2.00 mm (UK 14) crochet hook make 6 ch, ss into first ch to form a ring.

1st round: 1 ch, work 15 dc into ring, ss into first dc.

2nd round: (3 ch, tr2tog over next 2 dc, 3 ch, ss into next dc) 5 times placing last ss into first dc of previous round.

Fasten off.

to finish

Make a decorative tassel (see page 22) using all three yarn colours. Lightly press the chain lengths, then sew the ends to the back of the tassel binding.

Attach the flowers randomly around the length of the necklace, sewing them to the same colour chains.

Gorgeous corsage

The rich colours and glittering beads in this elegant corsage combine to make it the perfect pick-me-up for a plain or dark jacket.

Size
Flower with 3 rounds of petals measures 7.5 cm (3 in) across; half leaf measures 3 cm (1¼ in)

Materials
Rowan Wool Cotton
1 50 g ball in Main Shade (**MS**) /Gypsy 910
1 50 g ball in 1st Contrast (**1st C**) /Flower 943
Scottish Tweed 4ply
1 25 g ball in 2nd Contrast (**2nd C**) /Apple 015
Rowan Kidsilk Haze
1 25 g ball in 3rd Contrast (**3rd C**) /Blushes 583
1 25 g ball in 4th Contrast (**4th C**) /Jelly 597
3.50 mm (UK 9) crochet hook.
Tapestry needle
Beads to embellish flower
Beading needle and thread
Brooch pin finding

Tension
It is difficult to specify a tension on this pattern so simply work to the measurements given.

Abbreviations
1st C 1st Contrast
2nd C 2nd Contrast
3rd C 3rd Contrast
4th C 4th Contrast
ch chain
cm centimetres
dc double crochet
dtr double treble
htr half treble
in inches
mm millimetres
MS Main Shade
rep repeat
sp space
ss slip stitch
st(s) stitch(es)
tr treble

Flower

With 3.50 mm (UK 9) crochet hook and MS make 4 ch, ss into first ch to form a ring.

1st round: 1 ch, work 8 dc into ring, ss into first dc.

2nd round: 1 ch, 2 dc into each dc, ss into first dc. (16 dc)
Change to 1st C.

3rd round: 1 ch, *(1 dc, 1 htr, 1 tr) into first dc, (1 tr, 1 htr, 1 dc) into next dc, rep from * to end, ss into first dc. (8 petals)
Change to MS.

4th round: Working behind each petal, 1 ch, 1 dc into base of first dc, (3 ch, miss 5 sts, 1 dc into base of next dc) 7 times, 3 ch, ss into first dc.

5th round: ss into 3 ch arch, 1 ch, (1 dc, 1 htr, 3 tr, 1 htr, 1 dc) into each of the 8 3 ch arches, ss into first dc.
Change to 1st C.

6th round: Working behind each petal, 1 ch, 1 dc into base of first dc, (5 ch, miss 6 sts, 1 dc into base of first dc of petal) 7 times, 5 ch, ss into first dc.

7th round: ss into 5 ch arch, 1 ch, (1 dc, 1 htr, 5 tr, 1 htr, 1 dc) into each of 8 5 ch arches, ss into first dc.
Fasten off.

Half leaves (make 8)

With 3.50 mm (UK 9) crochet hook and 2nd C make 11 ch.

Working in a spiral, work 1 dtr into 5th ch from hook, 1 dtr into next ch, 1 tr into each of next 3 ch, 1 htr into next ch, 1 dc into last ch, 3 ch, working down other side of ch, work 1 dc into first ch, 1 htr into next ch, 1 tr into each of next 3 ch, 1 dtr into each of next 3 ch. Fasten off.

to finish

Sew in any loose ends.

With 3.50 mm (UK 9) crochet hook and 3rd C and working around the 2nd set of petals (5th round) on the flower, work 1 row of dc around each petal.

Sew the leaves to each corner of the last row of petals on the back of the flower. With 3.50 mm (UK 9) crochet hook and 4th C work 1 row of dc around all the leaves, working 3 dc into the points of the leaves.

Sew beads to the centre of the flower.

Sew the brooch pin finding to the back of the corsage.

Beautiful belt

This bold and beautiful hip belt will look cool worn with jeans or a flared summer skirt. Why not make one in colours to match both?

Materials
Rowan Handknit Cotton

• Colourway 1
1 50 g ball in Main Shade (**MS**) ecru/Ecru 251
1 50 g ball in 1st Contrast (**1st C**) palest brown/Linen 205
1 50 g ball in 2nd Contrast (**2nd C**) dark brown/Double Choc 315
3.50 mm (UK 9) crochet hook
Tapestry needle
2 lengths of leather string approximately 180 cm (70 in) long
Large beads in colours to match yarn

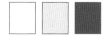

• Colourway 2
1 50 g ball in Main Shade (**MS**) green/Gooseberry 219
1 50 g ball in 1st Contrast (**1st C**) pale blue/Ice Water 239 205
1 50 g ball in 2nd Contrast (**2nd C**) dark blue/Turkish Plum 277
3.50 mm (UK 9) crochet hook
Tapestry needle
2 lengths of leather string approximately 180 cm (70 in) long
Large beads in colours to match yarn

Size
To fit average size adult

Tension
Each triangle measures 7.5 cm (2⅞ in).

Abbreviations
1st C 1st Contrast
2nd C 2nd Contrast
ch chain
cm centimetres
cont continue
dc double crochet
in inches
mm millimetres
MS Main Shade
rep repeat
sp space
ss slip stitch
tr treble

Triangle (make 12 or as many as needed to fit waist)

With 3.50 mm (UK 9) crochet hook and MS make 5 ch, ss into first ch to form a ring.

1st round (RS): 7 ch (counts as 1tr, 4 ch), (5 tr into ring, 4 ch) twice, 4 tr into ring, ss into 3rd of 7 ch.
Change to 1st C.

2nd round: ss into first 2 ch, 7 ch (counts as 1 tr, 4 ch), 2 tr into corner sp, *1 tr into each tr to corner, (2 tr, 4 ch, 2tr) into 4 ch sp, rep from * once more, 1 tr into each tr, 1 tr into same place as ss at end of 1st round, 1 tr into corner sp, ss into 3rd of 7 ch.
Change to 2nd C.

3rd round: 1 ch *(3dc, 1 ch, 3 dc) into 4 ch sp, 1 dc into each tr to next ch sp, rep from * to end, working last dc into same place as ss at end of 2nd round. ss into first dc.
Fasten off.

to finish

Sew in any loose ends.
Thread the triangles onto the leather string through each st of the 3rd round, making sure that the triangles face in alternate directions. Between each triangle make a knot, thread on a bead, then make another knot. Make sure you leave enough string at each end of the belt to fasten it.

Index

Acknowledgements

Publisher's acknowledgements
Executive Editor: Katy Denny
Editor: Leanne Bryan
Pattern Checker: Sue Horan
Executive Art Editor and Designer: Karen Sawyer
Photographer: Vanessa Davies
Props Stylist: Sorcha Bridge
Illustrator: Kuo Kang Chen
Senior Production Controller: Martin Croshaw
Picture Research: Sophie Delpech

The publisher would like to thank the following for the
loan of props for photography:
Flax PR www.flaxpr.com +44 (0) 20 7486 4242
Laura Ashley www.lauraashley.com +44 (0) 871 230 2301
Nougat www.nougatlondon.co.uk +44 (0) 20 7323 2222
Toast www.toastbypost.co.uk +44 (0) 870 240 0460
Pure www.purecollection.com +44 (0) 870 60 90 454

Author's acknowledgements
Thank you to Ann Hinchcliffe for her patience and for her
help with the yarns. Thank you to all at Hamlyn for their help
and guidance with the book, and to Vanessa Davies, the
photographer, for making my designs look stunning. A big
thank you goes to my husband, Andy, for making it possible
for me to spend time on the book, and to my daughter,
Lauren, who makes it all worthwhile.